W9-DFM-499

Seven Natural Wonders of EUROPE

Michael Woods and Mary B. Woods

TWENTY-FIRST CENTURY BOOKS
Minneapolis

To William J. Rowe, M.D.

Twenty-First Century Books
A division of Lerner Publishing Group, Inc.
241 First Avenue North
Minneapolis, MN 55401 U.S.A.

Website address: www.lernerbooks.com

Library of Congress Cataloging-in-Publication Data

Woods, Michael, 1946–
Seven natural wonders of Europe / by Michael Woods and Mary B. Woods.
p. cm. — (Seven wonders)
Includes bibliographical references and index.
ISBN 978–0–8225–9072–9 (lib. bdg. : alk. paper)
1. Europe—Description and travel—Juvenile literature. I. Woods, Mary B. (Mary Boyle), 1946– II. Title.
D907.W67 2009
914—dc22 2008027604

Manufactured in the United States of America
1 2 3 4 5 6 – DP – 14 13 12 11 10 09

Contents

Introduction

People love to make lists of the biggest and the best. Almost twenty-five hundred years ago, a Greek writer named Herodotus made a list of the most awesome things ever built by people. The list included buildings, statues, and other objects that were large, wondrous, and impressive. Later, other writers added new items to the list. Writers eventually agreed on a final list. It was called the Seven Wonders of the Ancient World.

The list became so famous that people began imitating it. They made other lists of wonders. They listed Seven Wonders of the Modern World and Seven Wonders of the Middle Ages. People even made lists of undersea wonders.

People also made lists of natural wonders. Natural wonders are extraordinary things created by nature, without help from people. Earth is full of natural wonders, so it has been hard for people to choose the absolute best. Over the years, different people have made different lists of the Seven Wonders of the Natural World.

This book explores seven natural wonders from the continent of Europe. Like Earth as a whole, Europe has far more than seven natural wonders. But even if people can never agree on which ones are the greatest, these seven choices are sure to amaze you.

A Wonderful Continent

Europe is a small continent. Of the world's seven continents, only Australia has less land than Europe. However, Europe has a large population. Only Asia and Africa have more people than Europe. The total population of Europe is about 700 million.

Europe extends from the Mediterranean Sea in the south to the Arctic Ocean in the north. The Atlantic Ocean is Europe's western boundary. The Ural Mountains in Russia form Europe's eastern boundary.

Europe is divided into forty-eight countries. These nations include the world's smallest country, Vatican City. With only 109 acres (44 hectares) of land, it is smaller than most towns. Europe also includes the world's biggest country, Russia. Russia extends over 6.4 million square miles (17 million square kilometers) of land. Its western portion is in Europe. Its eastern portion is in Asia.

Wonderful Adventure

This book will take you on a tour of some of Europe's natural wonders. The first stop will be at Loch Ness in Scotland. Some people think a strange monster lives in the lake. The next stop will be at an undersea volcano in Iceland. Not long ago, the volcano erupted, forming a brand-new island. The tour will also visit the coast of Norway. Here, the ocean reaches into the shoreline like long, narrow fingers. At another stop on the tour, a giant white cliff towers above the sea. Other fascinating places are waiting in between these visits. Read on to begin your adventure.

Mons Klint, a white cliff, towers over the sea in Denmark.

1 Loch Ness

The sun shines across Loch Ness in northern Scotland. Many tourists visit this lake to look for the legendary monster in the lake's depths.

One summer day in 1933, George Spicer and his wife were driving past Loch Ness. This long, narrow lake is in northern Scotland. Suddenly, George Spicer slammed on the brakes. The car screeched to a stop. The Spicers could not believe their eyes. Crossing the road in front of their car was a strange creature. It looked like a dinosaur. It carried a small animal in its mouth.

As the Spicers watched in amazement, the creature waddled across the road. Then it disappeared into some bushes along the edge of Loch Ness. It left a trail of squashed bushes leading into the lake.

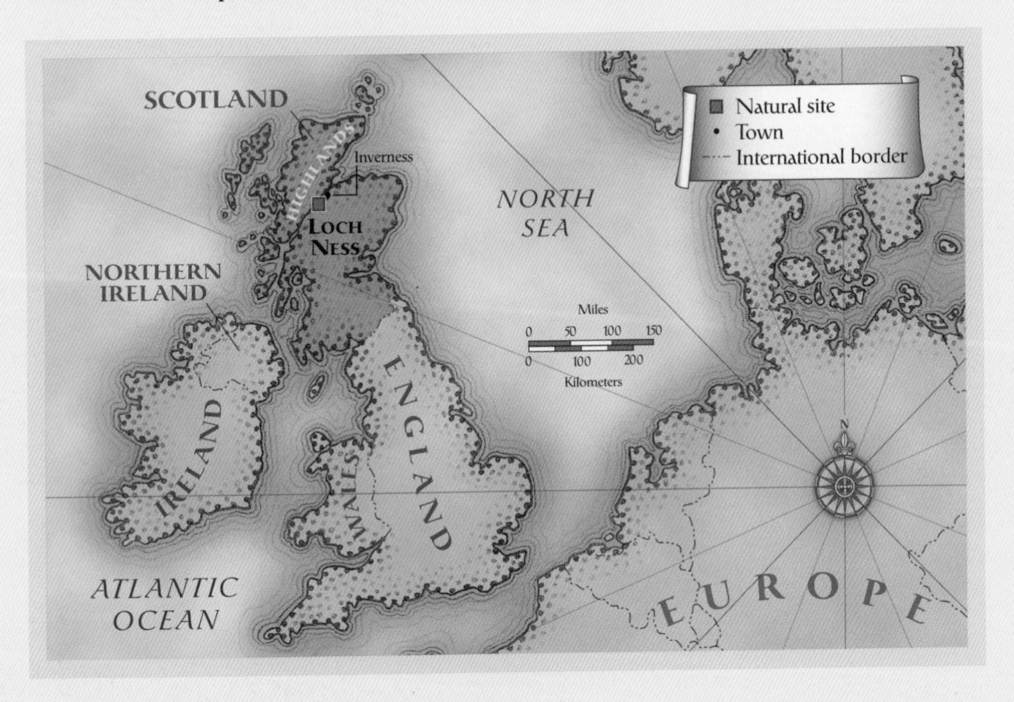

The Spicers told reporters that the animal was about 25 feet (8 meters) long—almost as big as a school bus. They said it had a long, skinny neck, about 12 feet (3.7 m) long.

Newspapers reported that the Spicers had seen a monster. People began calling it the Loch Ness monster, or Nessie for short. Soon, the Loch Ness monster had become world famous.

Lots of Lochs

Loch Ness is a large, deep freshwater lake. It sits southwest of the city of Inverness in northern Scotland.

The people of Scotland speak English, but they also use many words from a language called Scottish Gaelic. *Loch* is a Scottish Gaelic word meaning "lake." Therefore, Loch Ness simply means Lake Ness.

This aerial view of Loch Ness in Scotland shows how narrow it is. The lake is very deep however. It is 740 feet (230 m) at its deepest point.

Scotland is a land of lochs. More than 560 lochs are scattered throughout the country. Loch Ness is Scotland's second largest loch. It measures about 23 miles (37 km) long. The lake is very narrow. It is only about 1 mile (1.6 km) wide in most places.

Scotland's largest loch is Loch Lomond. This lake in central Scotland is 24 miles (39 km) long and 5 miles (8 km) across at its widest point. Even though Loch Lomond covers a larger area, Loch Ness holds more water. That's because Loch Ness is so deep. It reaches 740 feet (230 m) at its deepest point. That's about the distance from the top to the bottom of a seventy-five–story skyscraper.

Making a Loch

The northern part of Scotland is rugged and mountainous. It's called the Scottish Highlands because of the high hills and mountains. Between the mountains are deep, narrow valleys. Some of these valleys hold lakes, such as Loch Ness.

Scotland's lakes formed during the last ice age. This period began about 1.6 million years ago and ended about 11,500 years ago. During the ice age, Earth's climate was very cold. In Europe and other places, the land was covered by glaciers, or thick layers of ice.

Some glaciers were more than 10,000 feet (3,048 m) thick. They pressed down on the land with tremendous force. Sometimes, the heavy glaciers moved across the land. They slid on a thin layer of water beneath the ice. Like a snowball rolling over dirt, the glaciers picked up rocks as they moved. Some of the rocks were as big as houses. As the glaciers moved farther, the big rocks dug into the soil. In that way, the glaciers dug out deep valleys in Scotland and other places.

When the ice age ended, Earth's climate got warmer. The glaciers began to melt. Water from the melted ice filled the valleys. That's how Loch Ness and the other lochs formed in Scotland. The valley that holds Loch Ness is almost 1,500 feet (457 m) deep.

"I do not believe in the Loch Ness monster—yet—because there isn't enough evidence for it."

—Adrian Shine, Nessie investigator, 2007

The Pictish Dragon

After the ice age ended, people from other parts of Europe moved to Scotland. Early residents of the Scottish Highlands were farmers. They grew wheat, barley, cabbage, onions, and other crops. They also raised sheep, pigs, and cows. Women and children gathered wild plants to eat. The men hunted deer, wild pigs, rabbits, and other animals.

In A.D. 79, Roman armies invaded Scotland. At that time, the Romans had a powerful empire, based in modern-day Italy. The Romans found the Scottish Highlands occupied by fierce, warlike people. They liked to mark their skin with tattoos. The Romans called the inhabitants Picts, or "painted people."

The Picts carved pictures on slabs of stone. Then they placed the slabs upright on the ground. The carvings showed lifelike pictures of animals, including wolves, eagles, snakes, and fish.

One animal carved on the stones was strange and frightening. It looked like a dragon or seahorse. It had a long, narrow head and flippers instead of feet. Historians call the creature the Pictish Beast or Pictish Dragon. The Pictish Beast may have been an imaginary figure, like a modern-day cartoon. However, some people say it is an early drawing of the Loch Ness monster.

Pictish people carved this stone in the ninth century A.D. The carving in the middle shows the Pictish Beast.

Ever Wonder?

Who made the first Loch Ness monster sighting? It may have been Saint Columba, a religious man who spread Christianity among the Picts. In 565 Saint Columba was traveling near Loch Ness. He reported seeing a monster about to eat a man swimming in the loch. Columba said that he asked God's help in saving the man and the creature vanished.

This photo of Nessie ran in a British newspaper in 1934. About sixty years later, the photo was revealed to be a hoax.

Monster or Myth?

Scottish legends tell about "loch beasts" and "water horses" with magical powers. One legend describes an evil water horse that tricked children into riding on its back. Then the horse galloped into a loch, where the children drowned. Another story says that in A.D. 565, a religious man frightened away a sea monster near Loch Ness. After that encounter, nobody saw much of Nessie for hundreds of years.

Nessie sightings really picked up after the Spicers reported seeing the creature in 1933. The following year, a photograph appeared in a British newspaper. The picture showed a strange animal swimming in Loch Ness. The creature looked like a dinosaur. It swam with its head above water. Other people made still pictures and movies showing what looked like a monster swimming in Loch Ness.

In the late 1900s, people started to search the lake with sonar. Sonar is a device that uses sound waves to find objects underwater. Several expeditions searched the lake, but none of them found the monster.

Nessie's *Neighbors*

Whether or not the Loch Ness monster exists, a lot of other creatures live in and around Loch Ness. Fish live in the lake. Otters swim in the water and make their homes along the shore. Deer, rabbits, and squirrels live in the surrounding hills. The area is also home to blackbirds, woodpeckers, finches, partridges, and other birds.

"It was gray-brown, massive . . . the size of a bus, a big bus. It flipped over, just flipped right over like that, crashed down. You could see it, and the waves from that point were about three feet [1 m] high and ebbed to each side of the Loch."

—Ronald Mackintosh, describing a Nessie sighting from his youth, 1999

Many skeptics, or disbelievers, think there's no such thing as the Loch Ness monster. They think that people sometimes see tree branches floating in the water, waves on the lake, or reflections of objects on the surface and mistake them for sea monsters. Otters and other animals that live around Loch Ness could also be mistaken for monsters.

Some Loch Ness monster sightings are hoaxes, or tricks. For instance, in the early 1990s, an old man admitted that the 1934 Loch Ness monster newspaper photo was a fake. The man said that he and friends had made a fake sea monster out of wood and a toy submarine. They took "Nessie's" picture and sold it to the newspaper.

Hunting for Nessie

Stories about Nessie have made Loch Ness one of the most popular tourist attractions in Scotland. Thousands of people visit the area each year. They boat, swim, and fish in the lake. They also hike and drive through the

Tourists search for Nessie and other creatures on a day cruise on Loch Ness.

For *Peat's Sake*

If there is such a thing as Nessie, she could hide from people very easily in Loch Ness. The water in the lake is very cloudy. Soil in the land around Loch Ness contains a lot of peat. This fine, dustlike material comes from the remains of dead plants. Streams and rivers wash the peat into Loch Ness. Bits of peat float in the water, making it cloudy.

Loch Ness is seen behind Urquhart Castle in Scotland. Each year thousands of people visit the lake and surrounding area, some hoping to catch a glimpse of Nessie.

beautiful countryside surrounding Loch Ness.

Some visitors search for Nessie themselves. They take special "find-the-monster" boat cruises. The tour boats are equipped with sonar and special underwater cameras. Passengers can look at underwater images on TV screens as the boats sail around the loch. Visitor centers and museums near the lake also show movies and displays about Nessie.

The government of Scotland wants to keep tourists coming to Loch Ness. The tourists spend their money at hotels, restaurants, and other local businesses. The Scottish government has also passed laws protecting the loch and the surrounding countryside from pollution.

2 The Westmann Islands

Lava flows from the underwater volcano that created Surtsey Island, which is one of the Westmann Islands.

IN NOVEMBER 1963, A FISHING BOAT NAMED THE *ÍSLEIFUR II* WAS SAILING NEAR ICELAND. ICELAND IS AN ISLAND NATION IN THE NORTH ATLANTIC OCEAN. IT SITS BETWEEN GREENLAND AND NORWAY.

On November 14, the fishing crew saw black smoke in the distance. They thought that another ship had caught on fire and might be sinking. The *Ísleifur II* headed toward the smoke to rescue the ship's crew.

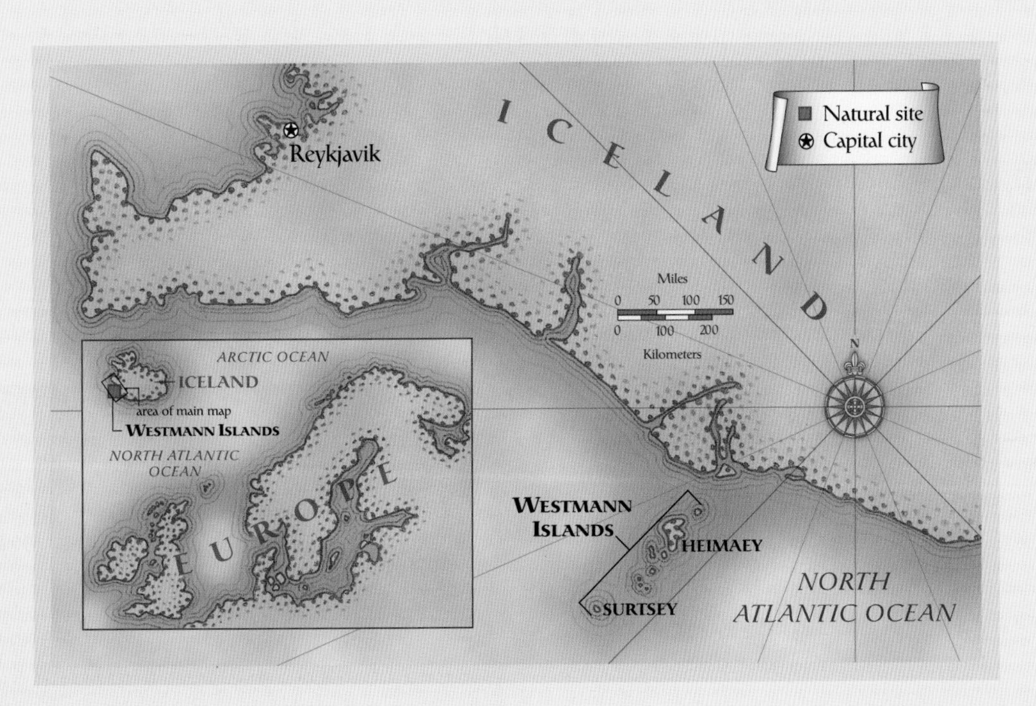

"The volcano was most vigorously active . . . and when darkness fell it was a pillar of fire and the entire cone was aglow. . . . Flashes of lightening lit up the . . . clouds and peals of thunder cracked above our heads."

—geologist Sigurdur Thorarinsson, describing the eruption that formed Surtsey, 1963

When the *Isleifur II* reached the smoke, crew members were surprised. The smoke was not coming from a sinking ship. It was coming from a volcano. A volcano is an opening in Earth's surface. Occasionally smoke, ash, and melted rock erupt, or burst, through the opening. The hot ash and rock pile up around the volcano, cool, and harden.

Many volcanoes erupt on land. But the volcano that the fishing crew found near Iceland was underwater. It sat on the floor of the Atlantic Ocean, about 425 feet (130 m) beneath the surface. Lava, or melted rock from the volcano, had been piling up, cooling, and hardening under the water. By the time the fishing crew arrived, the pile had almost reached the surface of the ocean.

Birth of New Earth

The volcano continued to erupt. The pile of lava rose higher and higher until it formed an island in the ocean. People in Iceland chose a name for the new island. They called it Surtsey. It was named after Surtur, the god of fire in ancient Icelandic legends.

Reporters and camera crews came to Iceland to watch the island grow. They broadcast pictures on television and printed stories in newspapers and magazines. Millions of people around the world followed the story.

The volcano erupted for almost three and a half years. Sometimes, smoke and ash from the eruption billowed 30,000 feet (9,146 m) into the sky. Surtsey got bigger and bigger.

From Iceland *to Hawaii*

Thousands of islands on Earth formed the same way Surtsey did. They rose up from undersea volcanoes. The Hawaiian Islands in the Pacific Ocean, for instance, are volcanic islands.

Top: *This photo from 1965 shows lava spewing from the undersea volcano that formed Surtsey.* Left: *After the volcano stopped erupting, the island of Surtsey remained above the water.*

FIRE *and Ice*

Although Iceland's volcanoes are hot and fiery, Iceland is a cold country. It is located far north on Earth, where the climate is very cold. About 15 percent of the country is covered in ice and snow year-round.

When the eruption finally ended on June 5, 1967, Surtsey was 555 feet (169 m) above the ocean. It covered an area of almost 1 square mile (2.5 sq km).

WEST MEN

Iceland is a very young land. It formed from volcanic eruptions during the last sixty thousand years. Most of Earth's other land formed about 4.5 billion years ago.

For thousands of years, Iceland was uninhabited. The first people to live on Iceland came from Norway. They arrived in A.D. 874. A Norwegian man named Hjörleifur Arnason brought Irish slaves to Iceland to help build the new settlement. The Norwegians called the Irish slaves West Men, because they came from the west.

The Irish slaves revolted. They killed Hjörleifur and escaped to a group of small islands off the coast of Iceland. Ingolfur Arnarson, Hjörleifur's brother, tracked down the runaway slaves and killed them. The modern Westmann Islands are named for these West Men. The name in Icelandic is Vestmannaeyjar.

In modern times, the Westmann Island group has fourteen islands—including Surtsey, the newest island. Only the largest island, Heimaey, is inhabited. The rest of the islands are wild land.

LAND OF FIRE

Surtsey is the youngest of the Westmann Islands. But the other islands are young too. They all formed during the last five thousand years. Five thousand

"This [volcano] . . . all burning and belching flame, stands in a perpetual blaze, which spreads over the mountain and wastes it inside and out."

—French writer and monk Herbert of Clairvaux, describing an Icelandic volcano, 1100s

years may seem like a long time. Compared to Earth's history, however, five thousand years is very short. Most of the land on earth formed millions of years ago.

All the Westmann Islands formed the same way Surtsey did. They bubbled up from lava released from undersea volcanoes.

Iceland is located on the Mid-Atlantic Ridge. The ridge is an undersea mountain range. It runs along the Atlantic Ocean floor for 9,300 miles (15,000 km), from Iceland to the tip of South America. The Mid-Atlantic Ridge is the meeting place of two tectonic plates. Tectonic plates are gigantic slabs of rock that form Earth's outer shell. The plates float on an underlying layer of magma—hot, melted rock.

At some places on Earth, tectonic plates are moving toward each other. In other places, tectonic plates are moving apart. Volcanoes often occur where two plates hit one another or spread apart. At the northern Mid-Atlantic Ridge, near Iceland, two plates are moving apart about 1.2 inches (3 centimeters) per year.

Iceland and the Westmann Islands sit above the Mid-Atlantic Ridge, which makes them a hot spot for volcanic activity. Heimaey Island in the Westmanns has a small town (below).

As they move, magma rises up from beneath the plates, creating volcanoes. When magma leaves a volcano, we call it lava.

Iceland also sits on a "hot spot," a place where great amounts of magma rise up from inside Earth. These two factors—the Mid-Atlantic Ridge and the hot spot—combine to give Iceland many volcanoes. It has about 130 volcanoes on land, with others beneath the surrounding ocean. Scientists say that Iceland's volcanoes have produced about one-third of all the lava ever released on Earth.

In addition to causing volcanoes, magma beneath Iceland also creates geysers. Geysers are hot springs that shoot jets of steam and hot water into the air. Geysers form when magma heats water under the ground. The heat turns the water into steam. The steam rises upward, pushing against water above it. When the pressure gets high enough, the geyser erupts. A stream of hot water shoots up from the ground.

ELDFELL

Volcanic eruptions can be destructive. In 1973 a volcano named Eldfell erupted on Heimaey, the only inhabited island in the Westmann Islands. Lava flowed through the island's main town (also named Heimaey) like a river of fire. The town's seven thousand residents had to leave to escape the lava.

NAMING THE *World's Geysers*

Geysers are found in many places on Earth. The geyser that gave all the world's geysers their name is located in Iceland. It is Geysir *(below)* in southwestern Iceland. In the Icelandic language, that name means "to erupt." Eruptions at Geysir sometimes shoot boiling-hot water almost 200 feet (60 m) into the air.

Above: *The Eldfell Volcano erupts on the Icelandic island of Heimaey in January 1973.* Below: *Houses on Heimaey burn in a lava flow. Heimaey is the only inhabited island in the Westmann Islands.*

To stop the lava, firefighters came up with a clever idea. They sprayed jets of water on the river of lava as it flowed through town. The water cooled the lava. As it cooled, the lava hardened. It turned rock-solid. It formed a dam that blocked the additional flow of lava through town.

Despite this success, the volcano still did extensive damage to the town. It buried more than four hundred homes, stores, and other buildings—about one-third of the city. The volcano erupted for five months. After it stopped, people were finally able to move back and rebuild their town.

Houses in Heimaey were covered with black lava after the Eldfell eruption of 1973.

Learning from Surtsey

Volcanic islands like Surtsey start out bare and lifeless. They are made out of ash and black, rock-hard lava. Soon, however, the islands teem with plants and animals. How does this change happen? By studying Surtsey, scientists were able to answer that question.

Even before the volcano stopped erupting, scientists began watching for the first signs of life on Surtsey. The first animal to arrive was a fly, which came in 1965. The fly probably came to Surtsey from Heimaey, about 11 miles (18 km) away. The first plant also appeared in 1965. It was a sea rocket, which grows on beaches and sand dunes. Its seeds probably floated across the ocean to Surtsey.

Volcanic ash is very fertile. Soon, more plants were taking root in the island's ashy soil. In 1970 seagulls began building nests and laying eggs on Surtsey. The birds' droppings made the volcanic soil even more fertile. More plants grew in the soil. Other birds followed the seagulls. Insects and more plant seeds arrived on the wind, water, and driftwood.

By the 1980s, Surtsey was greening up. Patches of grass and other plants were starting to carpet its surface. By the early 2000s—forty years after Surtsey emerged bare and lifeless from the ocean—the island was full of life. More than fifty types of plants were growing there. At least five kinds of birds were nesting there.

Children *to the Rescue*

Hundreds of thousands of puffins *(below)* build nests on the Westmann Islands every year. These seabirds are black and white. They have large, bright orange bills. In August, millions of newborn puffins leave their nests and head out to the ocean for a meal of fish. Sometimes, however, some birds fly in the wrong direction. They land on Heimaey Island. Children there collect the baby puffins in cardboard boxes. They release the puffins near the seashore.

Erosion is causing Surtsey to disappear. Waves, rain, and wind are wearing away the lava that formed the island.

Now You See It . . .

Surtsey is a nature preserve. The Icelandic government doesn't allow tourists to visit the island. Only scientists with special permission can go there. But even those people who are allowed to visit might not be able to do so for long. Surtsey is quickly disappearing. The lava that formed the island is soft and crumbly. Ocean waves, rain, and wind can easily wear it away. Part of the island has already crumbled away. Someday, the entire island may disappear.

Ever *Wonder?*

Does heat from Iceland's volcanoes have any practical use? Yes. Icelanders use the heat—called geothermal energy—in their homes and businesses. They pump water underground, where it gets boiling hot. A system of pipes then carries the hot water to homes, schools, and other buildings. People use some of the water for washing. They also use it to heat radiators that keep rooms toasty warm. Heating with geothermal energy is much cheaper than using natural gas, oil, or electric heat. In Iceland, 90 percent of homes use geothermal energy for heating.

This geothermal power station in Iceland sits inside a volcanic crater.

Even though tourists can't stop on Surtsey, they can visit Heimaey and the other Westmann Islands. In some places, ocean waves have carved out big caves along the island coasts. Tourists can sail into these caves in boats. They can also take whale-watching trips near the islands.

Tourists to Heimaey can visit the Pompeii of the North project. Pompeii was an ancient Roman city buried by a volcanic eruption. In modern times, scientists have dug away the lava and ash to make Pompeii visible again. Scientists are digging out some of Heimaey's buried buildings in the same way. Visitors can tour the buildings to see the volcano's damage.

3 The Jurassic Coast

The tall chalk cliffs of the Jurassic Coast contain rich deposits of fossils.

PEOPLE WALKING ALONG BEACHES OFTEN SEE SAND, SEASHELLS, AND SEAGULLS. ON THE BEACHES OF DORSET AND DEVON COUNTIES IN GREAT BRITAIN, PEOPLE MIGHT ALSO SEE THE REMAINS OF DINOSAURS!

This area of seashore is called the Jurassic Coast. The Jurassic period was a time in Earth's history from 213 to 145 million years ago. This was a time when dinosaurs lived on Earth. The remains of dinosaurs, as well as other prehistoric plants and animals, are still found here.

The Jurassic Coast stretches for 95 miles (153 km) along the English Channel. This body of water separates the island of Great Britain (which contains England, Wales, and Scotland) from France. The coast is lined by tall cliffs made of chalk and other minerals. It also holds one of the world's richest deposits of fossils. Fossils are the remains of animals and plants that lived millions of years ago.

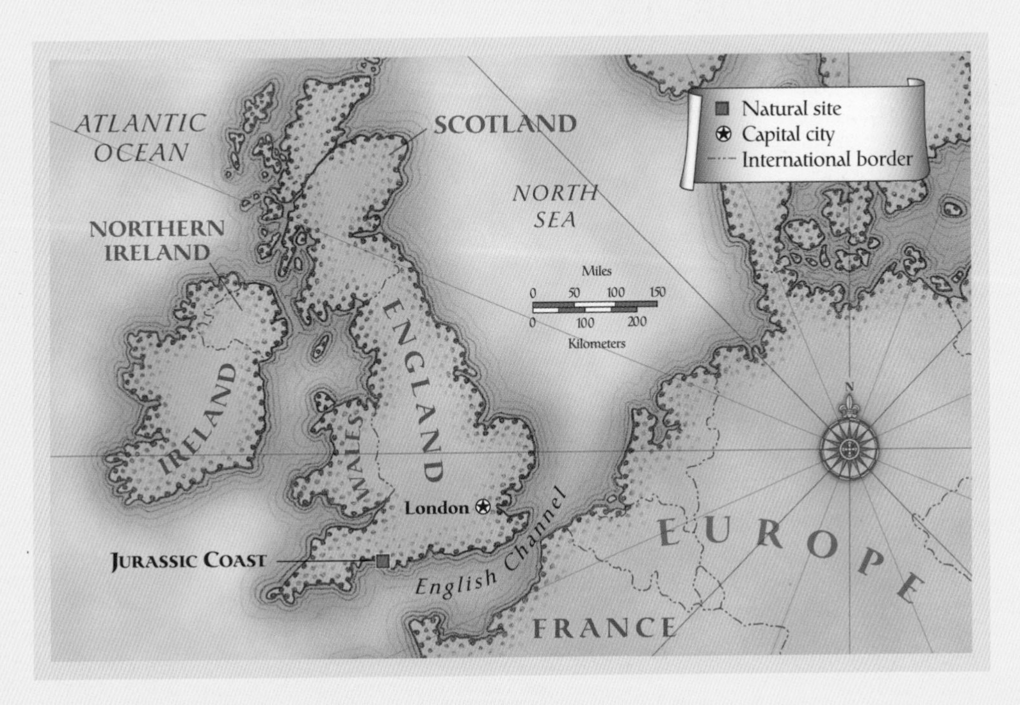

Forming Fossils

When an animal dies in the wild, its body normally disappears quickly. Other animals might eat the body, or it might just rot away. But if the dead animal is covered quickly by a layer of sand or mud, the body might become a fossil.

After this giant flying reptile died, its bones turned into fossils. The fossil is on display at the Natural History Museum in London, England.

Suppose a dinosaur died in a lake or river and was buried in mud under the water. The dinosaur's flesh would rot away. But the hard parts of the body—the bones, teeth, and claws—would remain under the mud. Over time, these hard parts might absorb minerals from the mud. The minerals would make the bones and other body parts as hard as rock. They would become fossils.

The Mesozoic Era

Dinosaurs lived on Earth during the Mesozoic era. This era began about 250 million years ago and ended about 65 million years ago. Scientists divide the era into three parts: the Triassic, Jurassic, and Cretaceous periods.

During the Triassic period, Earth's surface had just one continent. It was a huge landmass called Pangaea. Modern-day Great Britain was near the center of this supercontinent. Scientists think the land was hot and dry, like a desert.

Many kinds of animals and plants lived on Earth during the Triassic period. They included dinosaurs, flying reptiles, and reptiles that lived in the water. The first mammals also lived on Earth during this period.

At the end of the Triassic period, about 213 million years ago, Pangaea began to break into two pieces, Gondwanaland in the south and Laurasia in the north. The two landmasses slowly drifted apart.

During the next period, the Jurassic, the Atlantic Ocean began to form. Earth was warm at this time. The Jurassic Coast of Great Britain was hot, humid, and swampy.

Tracking *Prehistory*

Bones are not the only remains of dinosaurs on the Jurassic Coast. The dinosaurs have also left footprints along the coast. In the Purbeck area, visitors can see dinosaur tracks in the ground. The mud surrounding the tracks turned into stone millions of years ago, just like the bones of the dinosaurs themselves.

During the Cretaceous period, from about 140 million to 65 million years ago, Earth's big landmasses continued to break apart. Eventually, they formed Earth's seven continents. Dinosaurs were the largest land animals during this period. Dinosaurs and many other living things died out at the end of the Cretaceous period. After that, new kinds of life developed on Earth.

Fossils Revealed

For millions of years, the fossilized bones of dinosaurs and other creatures remained buried beneath the Jurassic Coast. Over time, more and more layers of mud and sand covered the fossils. Eventually, the mud and sand turned into rock. More and more layers piled up, forming high cliffs along the coast.

Gradually, waves, rain, and wind wore away parts of the cliffs. Sometimes, whole chunks of rock fell onto the beaches. The chunks contained dinosaur

This drawing from 1865 shows an ichthyosaur (left) *and a plesiosaur. Both reptiles once lived on the Jurassic Coast.*

"If you walk along the Dorset and East Devon coast you can walk continuously through . . . time for 180 million years. It's the only place on earth where you can do that."

—British geologist Denys Brunsden, 2001

Top: *This part of the Jurassic Coast is near Lyme Regis in Dorset County. The top of the cliffs are called the Golden Cap and are the highest point on the southern coast of Great Britain. The name comes from the golden-colored rock.* Left: *A close-up view shows rock layers in the cliffs along the coast in Dorset County.*

bones and other fossils that had been buried for millions of years. More than ten thousand years ago, people began living on Great Britain. Some of these people probably saw fossils on the beaches of the Jurassic Coast.

In the late 1600s, British scientists discovered the fossils at the Jurassic Coast. In the following centuries, fossil hunters came to the coast to collect and study the fossils.

She Sells Seashells by the Seashore

Mary Anning lived in the town of Lyme Regis in Dorset County. Lyme Regis was an especially good spot to hunt for fossils. The cliffs there held many fossils. During heavy rains, big chunks of rock often broke off the cliffs in big landslides, spilling fossils onto the beach.

Fossil hunter Mary Anning and a dog are shown on the coast in Dorset County. The painting is by an unknown artist and was made sometime before 1842.

When they were children, Mary and her brother Joseph hunted for fossils and sold them to collectors and tourists. In 1810 Joseph discovered a fossil that looked like the head of a crocodile. It was almost 4 feet (1.2 m) long. The following year, Mary found the creature's other bones.

Mary and Joseph had found the first complete skeleton of an ichthyosaur, a prehistoric marine (seagoing) reptile. The name ichthyosaur means "fish lizard." Ichthyosaurs lived during much of the Mesozoic era. These animals could grow to be 30 feet (9 m) long. They could weigh up to 2,000 pounds (910 kg). They had long, narrow jaws lined with sharp teeth. They also had big eyes and four fins.

As an adult, Mary Anning found other important fossils along the cliffs. In 1823 she uncovered the skeleton of a plesiosaur, another marine reptile. This name means "almost like a lizard." The plesiosaur was an odd-looking creature. It had a tiny head only 5 inches (13 cm) long. That head was attached to a long neck and a turtle-shaped body about 9 feet (3 m) long and 6 feet (2 m) wide.

In 1828 Anning found the complete skeleton of a flying reptile. It was the size of an eagle, with a wingspan of about 5 feet (1.5 m). The creature had wings covered with skin, much like a modern bat. It had huge jaws with two kinds of sharp teeth. Scientists named the creature *Dimorphodon*, which means "two forms of teeth."

One Piece at a Time

In the twentieth and twenty-first centuries, fossil hunters continued to make important finds along the Jurassic Coast. Starting in 2000, fossil hunters found bones of a dinosaur called *Scelidosaurus*. Different people found the bones one by one while walking on the beach. The last piece, completing the skeleton, was found in 2005. A museum in the British city of Bristol put the skeleton on display in 2008.

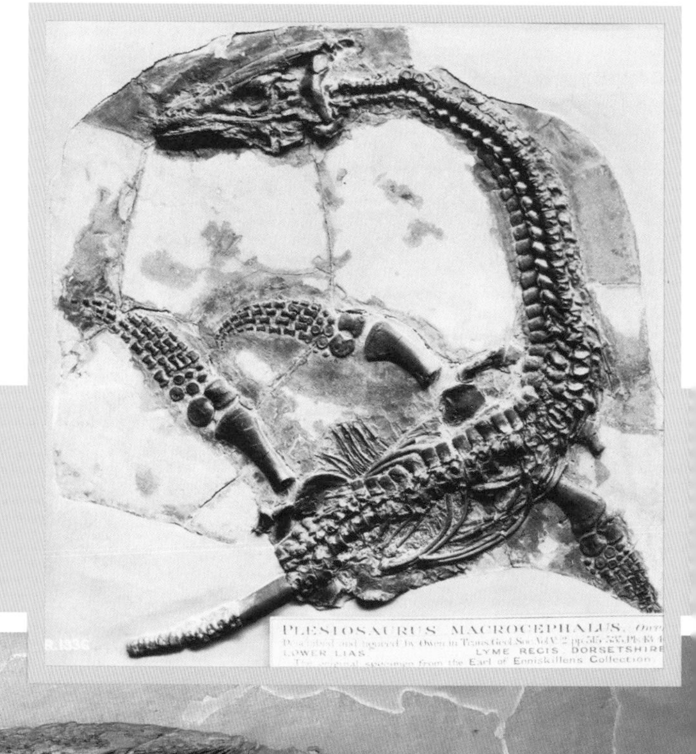

Right: ***Mary Anning found this plesiosaur fossil in 1823. It is on display at the Natural History Museum in London.*** **Below:** ***Ichthyosaurian fossils that Anning discovered are also on display at the museum.***

A fossil can be seen on a beach among the rocks along the Jurassic Coast.

Scelidosaurus lived 195 million years ago. It had big hind legs and two horns on the back of its head. It was small compared to many other dinosaurs. It measured about 13 feet (4 m) long and weighed 550 pounds (250 kg). *Scelidosaurus* was also an armored dinosaur. Its body was covered with bony plates. The plates protected *Scelidosaurus* from the teeth and claws of other dinosaurs that wanted to eat it. *Scelidosaurus* itself ate only plants.

Fresh Fossils

In 2001 the United Nations Educational, Scientific, and Cultural Organization (UNESCO) picked the Jurassic Coast as a World Heritage Site. World Heritage Sites are places of great importance to all humanity. UNESCO tries to protect and preserve these sites for future generations. The governments of Great Britain, Dorset, and Devon have also passed laws designed to conserve and protect the coast.

"There's a risk of rocks, coming down—the size of car engines, possibly the size of cars."

—Richard Edmonds, science manager for the Jurassic Coast World Heritage Site, 2008

Visitors comb the beach for fossils and hike to the top of one of the cliffs on the Jurassic Coast.

However, the Jurassic Coast is falling apart. Waves, rain, and wind constantly eat away at the cliffs. Sometimes, huge pieces of rock tumble down in a landslide. In 2008 a landslide occurred between the towns of Lyme Regis and Charmouth. A piece of cliff about 1,300 feet (400 m) long fell onto the beach. That's about as long as four high school football fields.

Fortunately, landslides do not damage the Jurassic Coast. Instead, they help it remain a natural wonder. Landslides bring fresh supplies of fossils to the beaches, allowing fossil hunters to make new discoveries.

Tourists are allowed to collect fossils at the Jurassic Coast. Thousands of tourists visit each year to do just that. Before taking the fossils home, however, fossil hunters must show them to officials. If someone has found an important fossil, officials will keep it for study and display in a museum.

Ever Wonder?

Why are people allowed to collect fossils on the Jurassic Coast? At many other natural wonders, tourists are supposed to look but not touch. Officials worry that people will damage the plants, animals, rocks, and other natural features if they handle them. But at the Jurassic Coast, people are encouraged to collect fossils. If left on the beach, the fossils will be smashed and washed away by waves. By collecting fossils for museums and private collections, tourists help preserve them.

This part of the Jurassic Coast has limestone formations. Wind and waves have created the unusual shapes.

Fossil Warden

Game wardens protect animals in national parks. The Jurassic Coast has a *fossil* warden. This official patrols the beaches near the towns of Charmouth and Lyme Regis. The warden reminds fossil hunters to let experts see their fossils before taking them home. The warden also reminds people not to go too close to cliffs, where they could be hurt by falling rocks.

4 The Black Forest

The Black Forest in southwestern Germany is not only filled with trees, but also has mountains, valleys, and villages.

IN THE FAIRY TALE "HANSEL AND GRETEL," A BROTHER AND SISTER GET LOST IN A FOREST. THE FAIRY TALE "SNOW-WHITE" ALSO TAKES PLACE IN A FOREST. "RAPUNZEL" IS A FAIRY TALE ABOUT A BEAUTIFUL GIRL WITH LONG HAIR. IN THIS STORY, A WICKED WITCH LOCKS RAPUNZEL AWAY IN A TOWER IN A FOREST.

These old fairy tales, and others like them, come from the European nation of Germany. German people told the stories for hundreds of years. In the early 1800s, the brothers Jacob and Wilhelm Grimm wrote the tales down. They published several books of German fairy tales. Like "Hansel and Gretel," "Snow-White," and "Rapunzel," many of the tales take place in an enchanted forest. The forest in the Grimms' fairy tales is based on a real place—the Black Forest in southwestern Germany.

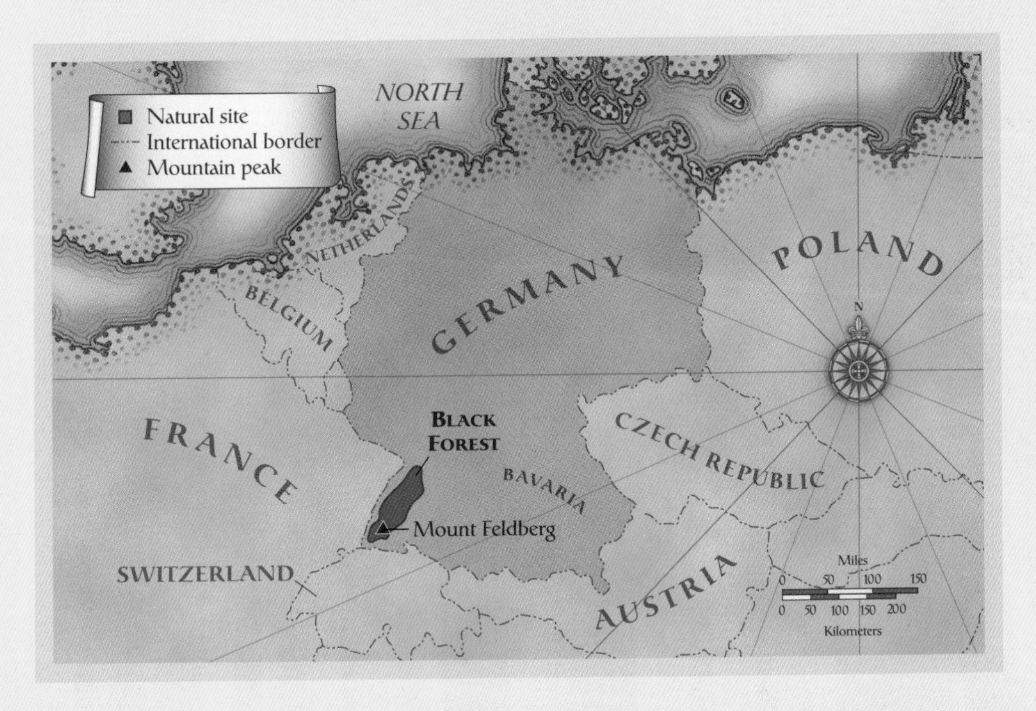

Dark and Spooky

A forest is a large area covered with trees. The Black Forest in Germany *is* filled with trees. But it also has mountains, valleys, villages, and farms. It is a big, rectangular-shaped region. It measures about 120 miles (200 km) from north to south and 37 miles (60 km) from east to west. That's about as big as the U.S. state of Connecticut.

The Black Forest got its name because it is dark and gloomy. Its trees grow very close together. Their dense leaves and branches keep sunlight from reaching the ground. Even on bright, sunny days, the forest floor is dim and shady.

Walking through the dark forest can be spooky. It's no wonder that people in earlier centuries thought the Black Forest was haunted. They thought that fairies, witches, and other magical creatures lived there. The forest made a perfect setting for fairy tales.

This view of the Black Forest, with early morning mist creeping through the trees, shows why some people think the forest is spooky.

Ever *Wonder?*

Who first used the name Black Forest? The ancient Romans may have been the first. When Roman soldiers marched into Germany in the first century B.C., they found their path blocked by a dark, dense forest. They called it the Silva Nigra ["black forest"] in their Latin language.

In the first century B.C., a Roman army traveled through the Black Forest. The general (later emperor) Julius Caesar led the army. Caesar wrote that strange animals lived in the Black Forest. He said that one animal looked like a horse. But it had a twisted horn growing from its forehead. Was it a unicorn?

Trees and Mountains

Southwestern Germany is a perfect place for a forest. It has rich soil and plenty of water. Numerous rivers flow through the land. The Danube River and the Rhine River are the most famous. Many lakes also dot the landscape. The Black Forest area gets a lot of sunshine, which helps trees grow.

The region has several mountains. Mount Feldberg is the highest. It rises about 4,900 feet (1,493 m) above sea level. Five other mountains are also more than 4,000 feet (1,219 m) high.

The mountain slopes in the Black Forest have mild winters and cool summers, good weather for evergreen trees. Evergreens are trees that do not lose their leaves in autumn. They stay green year-round. Many of the evergreen trees growing in the Black Forest are fir trees. The German word for "fir tree" is *tannenbaum*. People often cut down fir trees to use as Christmas trees. The German song "O, Tannenbaum" is about a Christmas tree.

Below the mountains, temperatures in the Black Forest are warmer. The soil and weather are just right for the growth of oak and beech trees. These trees are deciduous. Deciduous trees lose their leaves in autumn.

"The breadth of this . . . forest . . . is to a quick traveler, a journey of nine days. . . . Owing to its extent [it] touches the confines of many nations. . . . It is certain that many kinds of wild beast are produced in it which have not been seen in other parts."

—Roman general Julius Caesar, 50s or 40s B.C.

Evergreen trees fill the slopes of mountains in the Black Forest. Forest surrounds a village in the valley.

At Home in the Forest

Many animals live in the Black Forest. These include ordinary forest animals, such as eagles, owls, and squirrels. The forest also has some unusual creatures. One peculiar animal is the Baden worm. It is a giant, growing to a length of almost 24 inches (61 cm). The worm digs tunnels 8 feet (2.5 m) deep into the ground.

In between wooded areas, many people operate farms in the Black Forest. Some farmers raise cows and sheep. Others raise Black Forest foxes. These animals aren't really foxes. They are actually workhorses, originally used to pull logs out of the forest. These horses are strong but gentle.

The Black Forest is also a home for people. Some Black Forest villages are hundreds of years old. They have picturesque shops, churches, and other buildings.

Going, Going . . .

Scientists think that the Black Forest formed about ten thousand years ago, after the last ice age. In Europe the climate warmed up and the glaciers melted. Trees and other plants were able to grow in the warm soil.

A vast forest grew across central Europe. It stretched for hundreds of miles, from Germany and Switzerland in the west to Romania in the east. The Romans called it the Hercynian Forest. The Black Forest formed the western side of the Hercynian Forest.

Over the centuries, people cut down trees in the Hercynian Forest. They used some of the wood to build houses. They burned other wood for cooking and heating. People also cut down trees to clear land for farming.

Little by little, people cut down most of the Hercynian Forest. In modern times, the Black Forest is one of the few remaining parts of that great woodland.

Left: ***The Black Forest fox is a kind of horse that was once used to pull logs out of the forest.*** **Below:** ***Baden-Baden is just one of the picturesque towns of the Black Forest.***

WORRIES ABOUT THE WONDER

In the twenty-first century, the Black Forest faces many threats. For instance, some people still cut down trees in the forest. They use the wood for building.

Air pollution also hurts the forest. High in the air, pollution from factories and cars mixes with rainwater. The water becomes acidic, or sour, sort of like lemon juice. When this "acid rain" falls, it damages trees and other plants. Scientists estimate that acid rain has damaged up to half of all trees in the Black Forest.

Nature also has damaged the forest. In 1999 a fierce winter storm swept through France, Switzerland, and Germany. Winds reached 162 miles (260 km) per hour. The wind knocked down thousands of trees in the Black Forest.

The German people want to preserve and protect the Black Forest. Germany has passed laws limiting logging in the forest. It also tries to reduce air pollution that causes acid rain.

The Black Forest is a national and international treasure. Thousands of tourists visit the area each year. They help the economy by spending money at restaurants, shops, and hotels. The forest has about 14,000 miles (23,000 km) of trails. Tourists hike, bike, and ski on the trails. Some visitors canoe on the forest's lakes and rivers. Others stroll through seventeenth- and eighteenth-century villages.

BLACK FOREST *Cake*

A delicious dessert is named for the Black Forest. Black Forest cake is very popular in Germany, Austria, and other countries. It contains several layers of chocolate cake, with whipped cream and cherries in between. More whipped cream, cherries, and chocolate shavings adorn the top of the cake.

"[In winter] . . . the Black Forest is not even dark. It is dazzlingly, brilliantly white with snow . . . the woods appear [blue] as they reflect the color of the sky. That is the Black Forest at its best."

—U.S. writer John Dornberg, 1986

Above: *Snowboarders enjoy the view from a mountain in the Black Forest. Visitors flock to the Black Forest in all seasons to take advantage of the beautiful scenery and many activities.*
Left: *Many trees in the Black Forest have been damaged by acid rain.*

5 Mons Klint

The chalky surface of Mons Klint in Denmark rises above the waters of the Baltic Sea.

If you've ever written on a blackboard with chalk, you know that chalk is bright and white. Imagine a giant cliff made of chalk. It would gleam white in the sun. That's exactly what you'll see if you visit Mons Klint in Denmark. Mons Klint is a long, tall cliff on the Danish island of Mon.

Denmark is a country in northern Europe. It sits just north of Germany. Most of the nation is a peninsula, a piece of land that juts out into the water. In this case, the surrounding water is the North Sea to the west and the Baltic Sea to the east. In addition to this mainland, Denmark includes almost five hundred islands. The island of Mon is east of the Danish mainland. It is near Zealand, Denmark's largest island and the location of its capital city, Copenhagen.

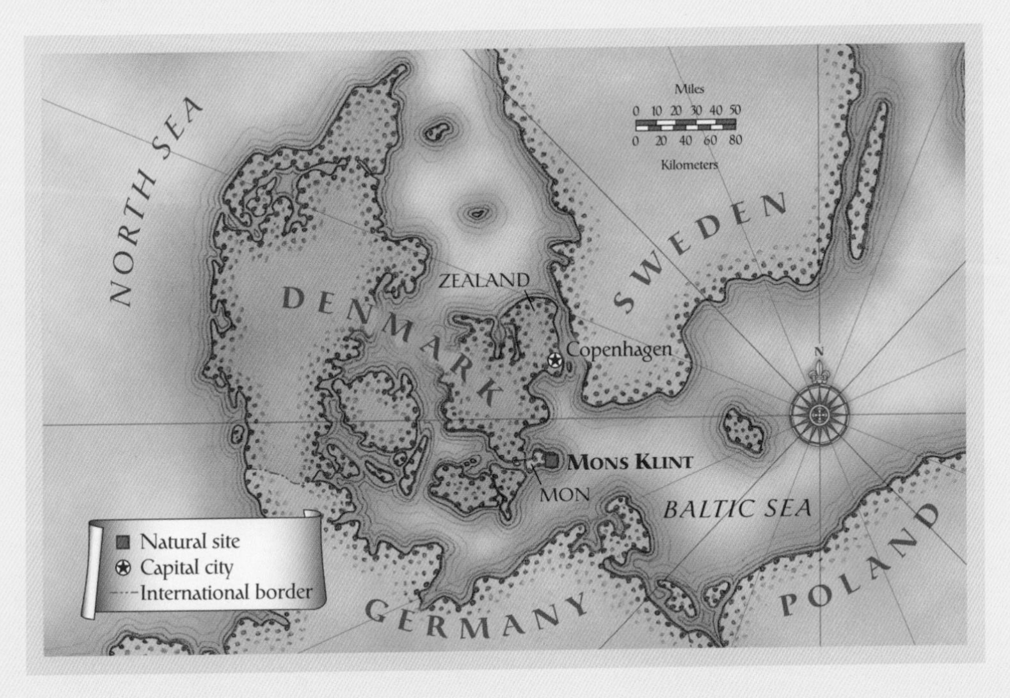

"The sound of the waves reflecting from the high, white cliffs, the impressive views, the conscience of walking in a landscape with a geology created at the time of the dinosaurs . . . everything is special and fantastic."

—Danish writer Erik Pontoppidan, 2003

The Danish word for "cliff" is *klint*. Mons Klint, therefore, means "cliff of Mon." The cliff runs for almost 4 miles (6.4 km) along the coast of Mon.

Denmark is a lowland area. Most of its land is only 100 feet (30 m) above sea level. But the cliff at Mons Klint is 400 feet (122 m) high—almost as high as a forty-story building. From a distance, the cliff is a fantastic sight. It gleams bright white in the sun. The white face contrasts sharply with the deep blue water of the Baltic Sea.

This aerial view of Mons Klint shows the cliff shining white against the dark green forest and blue water of the Baltic Sea.

Fossil Hunters

Sometimes people walking along the beach at Mons Klint find fossils lying among the chalk. Fossils are the remains of ancient plants and animals. The fossils at Mons Klint come from plants and animals that lived millions of years ago, when Denmark was covered by an ocean. When the plants and animals died, their remains fell to the seafloor. They were buried in the piles of calcium carbonate that eventually turned into chalk.

From Coccolithophores to Chalk

The chalk cliff at Mons Klint started out as tiny plants called coccolithophores. These plants are so small that you could line up 250 of them on a grain of sand. The plants have shells, or outer skeletons. The shells act like armor plating to protect the plants.

Coccolithophores float in the ocean. To build their shells, they collect a mineral from the water. That mineral is calcium carbonate. When coccolithophores die, they sink to the seafloor. Their bodies rot away and disappear. However, their calcium carbonate shells remain.

Over time, calcium carbonate shells pile up on the seafloor. At first, the layers are soft like mud. Over millions of years, more and more layers build up. The weight from above packs the calcium carbonate tightly together. It gradually changes. The original muddy material becomes a soft rock—chalk.

This colored micrograph shows the fossil of a coccolithophore of the same sort found at Mons Klint.

The Age of Chalk

The chalk layers that grew into Mons Klint began to form about 140 million years ago, during the Cretaceous period. That name comes from a Latin word, *creta,* which means "chalk." The

Cretaceous period ended about 65 million years ago.

During the Cretaceous period, Earth's surface looked very different than it does in modern times. The continents were in different locations. Africa, South America, Australia, and Antarctica were all stuck together. They were part of a "supercontinent" called Gondwanaland. Gondwanaland contained 70 percent of Earth's land.

The oceans also were different. They were larger, covering more of Earth than the modern oceans. All of the lands of western Europe were submerged under warm ocean water. That warm water was a perfect place for coccolithophores to grow. In several places in Europe, their skeletons piled up and formed chalk deposits.

About ten thousand years ago, sea levels dropped. That left the chalk beds sticking up above the water. Mons Klint is one of those chalk beds. Others are the chalk cliffs at the Jurassic Coast and the White Cliffs of Dover in Great Britain and the cliffs of Rugen Island in Germany.

TEACHING *with Chalk*

When your parents and grandparents went to school, every classroom had a blackboard, or chalkboard. The blackboard was made of black slate. Teachers used chalk to write and draw on the blackboard. The process was a little messy. Chalk dust got on people's fingers and clothing. Teachers used big cloth erasers to clean chalk off the blackboards. Students took turns thumping erasers together to shake out the chalk.

The White Cliffs of Dover, in England, are another example of chalk cliffs.

"Mons is mostly known by its incredible nature, all kinds of landscapes are found here such as beech woods, moors, forests of reed, salt meadows. . . ."

—Danish writer Majbritt Levinsen, 2007

King of the Mountain

The first people arrived in Denmark soon after the ocean levels dropped. They came from Germany and other parts of Europe. Most lived in small farming and fishing villages.

Warrior-sailors called Vikings lived in Denmark, Norway, and other parts of northern Europe. A Viking leader named Harold Bluetooth united Denmark into a single kingdom about A.D. 958.

Danish people told many stories about Mons Klint. One story said that the King of the Mountain lived in the cliff. He carved two caves into the soft rock. One cave was his home. The other cave was a home for his dog and white horse. Stories said that as long as the king ruled, no enemy could conquer Denmark. If an enemy invaded, the story said, the king could turn trees from the forests and stones from the beaches into soldiers.

Finding Flint

In ancient times, people crushed chunks of chalk from Mons Klint to look for flint. This hard, dark-colored stone forms inside chalk deposits. Like chalk, it comes from the skeletons of sea animals. Ancient people used flint from Mons Klint to make knives, axes, and other tools and weapons. People even used flint as money. They traded pieces of flint for other goods.

Worries about the Wonder

Nature is the biggest threat to Mons Klint. The chalk cliff is very soft. Rain, wind, and ice can easily erode (wear away) the chalk. Scientists estimate that a slice of the cliff face, about ½ inch (1 cm) thick, crumbles off each year.

Sometimes, landslides occur on the cliff. During a landslide, a whole section of chalk

Tourists check out the beach below Mons Klint. The beach is dotted with chalk stones that have broken off the cliff.

suddenly breaks off. One of the biggest landslides happened in 2007. About 1,000,000 pounds (450,000 kg) of chalk tumbled into the sea.

Mons Klint is a popular tourist attraction. About 300,000 people visit the cliff every year. Visitors can enjoy a spectacular view from the top of the cliff. There are marked paths for hiking and biking. The shore below Mons Klint is one of Denmark's most popular beaches.

The Danish government owns large areas of the cliff and surrounding lands. Government rules protect and preserve this natural wonder. For instance, people are not allowed to build houses or other buildings on the cliff. The rules will help to preserve this natural wonder far into the future.

Visitors can look down from the top of Mons Klint to see a view of the Baltic Sea and surrounding area.

6 Fjords of Norway

A village is nestled in the fjords in Norway.

THE EUROPEAN COUNTRY OF NORWAY IS A LAND OF NATURAL WONDERS. IT EVEN HAS NATURAL WONDERS INSIDE ITS NATURAL WONDERS!

Norway's most famous natural wonders are its fjords. Fjords are long, narrow valleys with steep sides. Unlike other kinds of valleys, however, fjords open onto the sea on one end. That means fjords are filled with ocean water. On a map, Norway's fjords look like long skinny fingers of water reaching into the coastline. Some fjords stretch inland for more than 100 miles (160 km).

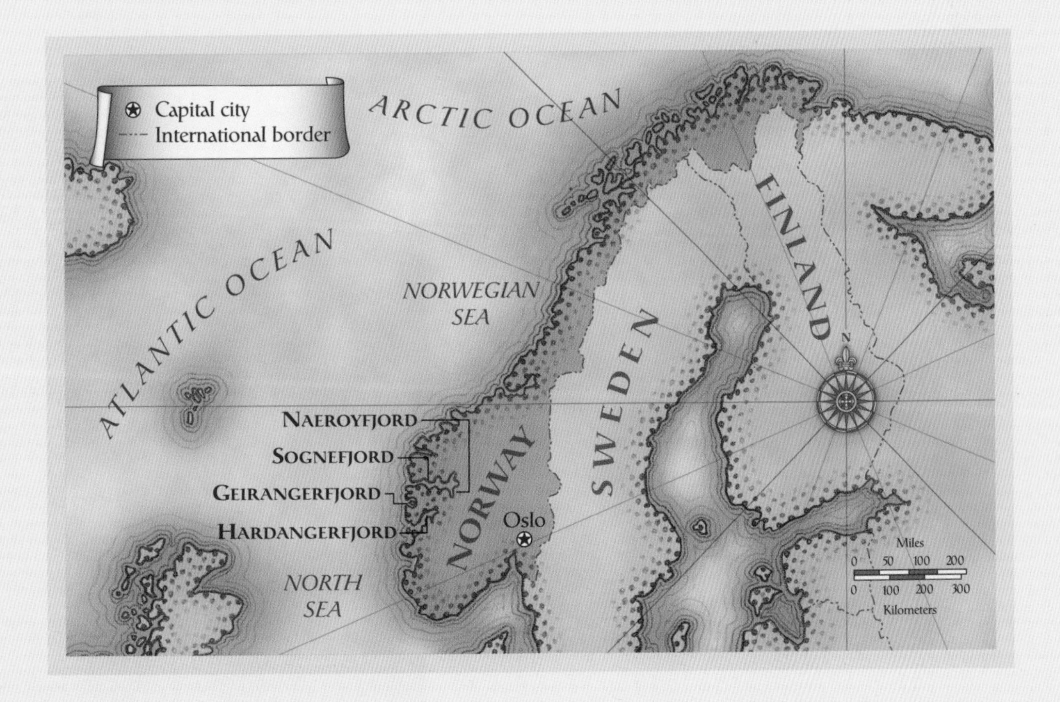

"Their exceptional natural beauty is derived from their narrow and steep-sided . . . rock walls. . . . The sheer walls of the fjords have numerous waterfalls whole free-flowing rivers cross their . . . forests to glacial lakes, glaciers and rugged mountains."

—*UNESCO*, 2005

Norway is one of the northernmost countries in Europe. Its name means "northern way." It is a rugged land, with forests, mountains, and valleys. To the east, Norway shares a border with Sweden. To the west, it borders the North Atlantic Ocean. The fjords along Norway's coastline are inlets of the ocean. Norway has thousands of fjords.

Norway is not the only place with fjords. The western coast of North America, between Alaska and Washington State, has many fjords. Fjords also line the coasts of New Zealand, South America, Antarctica, and Greenland.

Wonders Inside Wonders

Norway has two of the world's longest fjords. Sognefjord in southern Norway is 126 miles (203 km) long. Hardangerfjord, also in the south, is 111 miles (179 km) long. Only one other fjord is longer. It is Scoresby Sound in Greenland. At 280 miles (451 km) long, it is the longest fjord in the world.

In many places in Norway, smaller fjords branch off from the big fjords. On a map, the small fjords look like branches on a tree trunk. Sognefjord has a branch named Naeroyfjord. It is the narrowest fjord in the world. At one point, its sides narrow to a width of only 829 feet (250 m). Along those sides, mountains tower 5,906 feet (1800 m) above the water.

Fjord Fairy Tale

The famous folktale "Three Billy Goats Gruff" began along the fjords of Norway. The story tells about three goats that want to cross a bridge. However, a terrible troll lives under the bridge. He threatens to eat the goats if they try to cross. The oldest and largest goat finally knocks the troll into the river and makes the bridge safe.

Top: *A ship sails near Hardangerfjord. It is one of the longest fjords in Norway.*
Left: *Mountains tower over Naeroyfjord, the narrowest fjord in the world.*

Geirangerfjord is famous for its stunning waterfalls. In these places, water from rivers and streams plunges over the side of the fjord. At one spot, two waterfalls face one another across Geirangerfjord. On one side is the Seven Sisters. This waterfall contains seven separate streams of water. Across the fjord from the Seven Sisters is a single, larger waterfall. People call it the Suitor. A suitor is usually a man who wants to marry a woman. People who named the Suitor imagined that it was in love with one of the Seven Sisters. Another waterfall on Geirangerfjord is called the Bridal Veil. Its water streams gently over the edge of a cliff. When sun shines through the waterfall, it looks like a delicate head covering (veil) for a bride.

Fjord *Horse*

Norway has a famous breed of horse called the fjord horse *(below)*. Fjord horses are small but very strong. For hundreds of years, farmers in western Norway used fjord horses to pull plows and heavy wagons.

Forming Fjords

Norway's fjords formed during the last ice age. That period began about 1.6 million years ago. Earth became colder. In Europe, snow and ice piled up into huge glaciers. Some of the glaciers were 2.5 miles (4 km) thick.

The glaciers pressed down on the ground with tremendous force. They moved slowly over the land. As the glaciers moved, they ground away the land below them. In Norway, moving glaciers carved deep valleys. When the last ice age ended, about 11,500 years ago, the valleys filled with seawater. They became fjords.

"The fjords of Norway . . . are an incomparable wonder region."

—U.S. writer Henry R. Armstrong, 1927

The Seven Sisters waterfalls are separate streams that fall over the Geirangerfjord in Norway. The Suitor and the Bridal Veil are other waterfalls in this fjord.

Norwegians—Ancient and Modern

People began moving into Norway from other parts of Europe right after the ice age ended. The first Norwegians moved from place to place. They hunted wild animals, fished, and gathered plants for food.

Some of the most famous early Norwegians were Vikings. They were warriors, pirates, and traders. Their name comes from Vik, a large bay in

Right: ***Vikings from Norway are shown at sea in this woodcut from the book*** **The Romance of Discovery—A Thousand Years of Exploration and the Unveiling of Continents.** ***The book was published in 1897.*** **Below:** ***Vikings and other early Norwegians lived near the fjords and used them for fishing and transportation.***

This colorful village is on Nusfjord. Many villages nestle along the fjords. Tourists often visit them on sightseeing cruises.

southern Norway. From their bases in Norway, Sweden, and Denmark, Vikings raided villages in other parts of northern Europe. They flourished from the late A.D. 700s to about 1100.

After the Viking period ended, Norwegians lived a more settled life. They built towns and farms. Often, Norwegians built their towns at the end of fjords. Townspeople fished in the fjords. They also sailed boats down the fjords to the sea.

In modern times, the old Norwegian villages look like something out of a storybook. They have cobblestone streets lined with old-fashioned homes, shops, and restaurants. In many places, farms and orchards surround the villages. Cows graze peacefully on green mountain slopes nearby.

Many visitors to Norway take boat trips up fjords. This kind of trip is a real treat. First you enjoy the beautiful deep-blue water, lapping against steep, rocky cliffs. Then, rounding a bend, you might see a picturesque village come into view.

Ever *Wonder?*

Have people found any use for Norway's fjords? Some Norwegian people work *in* the fjords. They earn a living by fishing. Some fish in the traditional way, with nets and lines. Others operate fish farms. At fjord fish farms, people raise fish in cages underneath the water. Norway's fish farms produce more than 88 million pounds (40 million kg) of salmon and rainbow trout each year.

People have set up fish farms in the deep waters of the fjords.

Cruise ships sit in an inlet near Geirangerfjord. The fjord is a UNESCO World Heritage Site.

Protecting the Wonder

The fjords are one of Norway's most popular tourist attractions. Thousands of people visit these natural wonders each year. Tourists sail up fjords on boat cruises and take helicopter rides over the fjords.

The Norwegian government tries to protect the fjords from damage. For example, people are not allowed to build factories that might pollute water in the fjords. In 2005 UNESCO selected two Norwegian fjords—Geirangerfjord and Naeroyfjord—as World Heritage Sites.

Despite this protection, nature itself threatens some of the fjords. Scientists are especially concerned about Geiranger Fjord. The fjord sits alongside Akerneset Mountain. The mountain is made from soft stone and loose soil that is slowly crumbling. One day, the mountain could tumble into the fjord, damaging its natural beauty and destroying nearby buildings. Fortunately, most other Norwegian fjords are safe from such danger. They are likely to be wondrous for years to come.

7 THE Alps

Mont Blanc, the highest mountain in the Alps, rises above a snow- and tree-covered valley.

EVERY ONCE IN A WHILE, A NATURAL WONDER IS SO AMAZING THAT IT TURNS PEOPLE INTO COPYCATS. PEOPLE FAR AWAY BORROW ITS NAME FOR WONDERS IN THEIR OWN COUNTRY. THE ALPS, A LARGE MOUNTAIN RANGE IN EUROPE, IS THAT KIND OF NATURAL WONDER. MENTION THE WORD *ALPS*, AND PEOPLE IMMEDIATELY THINK OF TOWERING MOUNTAINS.

The name Alps comes from *alb,* an ancient word meaning "mountain." The Alps in Europe were the first mountains called Alps. Later, people in Australia named their highest mountains the Australian Alps. In the United States, the San Juan Mountains in Colorado (part of the Rocky Mountains) are sometimes called the American Alps. The first European settlers in western Canada used the name Canadian Alps for the Canadian Rocky Mountains.

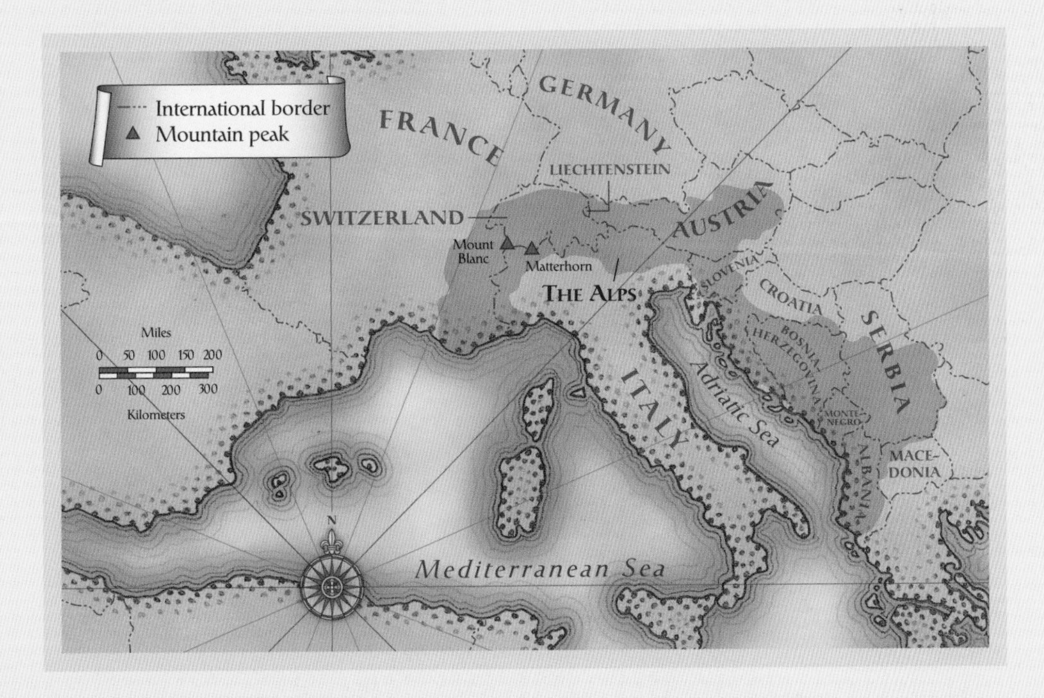

The highest mountain in the Alps is Mont Blanc. The mountain is on the border between Italy, France, and Switzerland.

The word *Alps* has led to even more words. *Alpine* refers to anything connected with lofty mountains. For instance, alpine flowers are flowers that grow on high mountain slopes. Alpine villages are settlements in the mountains. An alpinist is someone who climbs tall mountains.

Highs and Lows

The Alps are located in south-central Europe. They extend for 750 miles (1,207 km) across the continent. That's about the distance between Chicago, Illinois, and New York City.

On the west, the Alps begin in southern France. They continue eastward into Switzerland, Liechtenstein, northern Italy, and Austria. Then the Alps curve southeastward into Slovenia, Croatia, Bosnia-Herzegovina, Serbia, and Montenegro. In the south, the Alps end in Albania, on the coast of the Adriatic Sea. The Alps cover more than 80,000 square miles (207,000 sq. km)

The Alps vary in height. The lowest peaks measure about 4,593 feet (1,400 m). The highest mountain is Mont Blanc, on the border between Italy, France, and Switzerland. It measures 15,771 feet (4,807 m) high. The air at this height is very cold, even in summer. Mont Blanc is capped with snow year-round. Its name means "white mountain" in French.

The Matterhorn, on the border between Switzerland and Italy, is another famous Alpine peak. It is shaped like a pyramid, with a broad base and sides that narrow to a point at the top. The Matterhorn towers to a height of 14,692 feet (4,478 m). Its interesting shape and great height make it famous.

The Matterhorn is a famous mountain in the Alps, on the border between Switzerland and Italy. Its pyramid shape is reflected in a lake nearby in this photo.

Mountain Waters

Many high mountains in the Alps have glaciers. These huge ice sheets have formed because the air is so cold on top of tall mountains. Because of their great weight, glaciers slowly flow down mountainsides. As the glaciers encounter warmer weather at lower altitudes, some of the ice melts. Melting water from glaciers, and from mountain snows, forms streams that tumble down through the Alps.

The streams eventually combine to become Europe's big rivers. For instance, water flowing down from the Alps creates the Rhone River. It flows for 505 miles (813 km) through France and Switzerland. Water from the Alps also forms the Rhine River. It flows for 820 miles (1,320 km) through western Europe. The Po River in Italy also begins in the Alps.

Left: ***The Altesch Glacier in Switzerland is the largest glacier in the Alps.*** **Right:** ***A stream bubbles down a mountain in the French Alps.***

"The crests of the Alps and the parts near the passes are completely treeless and bare of vegetation because of the snow which lies there continually . . . but the slopes half-way down . . . are grassy and well-wooded."

—Greek historian Polybius, 100s B.C.

This part of the Swiss Alps has forested valleys with meadows.

Mountains of Life

The Alps are the most densely populated mountainous area in the world. More than 20 million people live near these mountains. Some of the people are farmers. Others live in big cities beneath the mountains.

The Alps are a good place to live for several reasons. First, the fertile soil is excellent for farming. The climate is also pleasant year-round. Most important, water is plentiful. People use the water that flows down alpine slopes for drinking, cooking, and bathing. Farmers use the water to irrigate crops. Rivers that flow down from the Alps are also highways for shipping products to market. Fast-flowing Alpine rivers also provide people with power. The water spins machines called turbines. The spinning turbines produce electricity. Power lines carry the electricity to cities and towns throughout Europe.

The Alps also provide a playground for millions of visitors. In winter people come from all over the world to ski and enjoy other sports in the Alps. Several times, cities in the Alps have hosted the Winter Olympic Games. In summer, tourists hike and visit quaint mountain towns. Adventurers come to climb the Matterhorn and other peaks. Restaurants, hotels, and other tourist businesses provide jobs for local residents.

People aren't the only residents of the Alps. The mountains provide a home for wild plants and animals. Some mountain slopes have forests of oak, beech, ash, pine, and other trees. Beautiful wildflowers bloom in meadows in spring and summer. Owls, golden eagles, and other birds soar through the Alpine skies. Large animals also find a home here. Among them are the Alpine ibex, a wild goat with large curved horns, and a goatlike creature called the chamois.

Look Out *Below*

Snow in the Alps can be dangerous. The snow can suddenly tumble down the mountains in an event called an avalanche. The fast-moving river of snow can bury skiers and crush houses and other buildings.

Skiers glide down the slopes at a ski resort in the Alps in Austria. Visitors come to the Alps year-round to enjoy skiing, hiking, and other sports.

Woof, Woof Pass

Saint Bernards are very large dogs. They can weigh more than 220 pounds (100 kg) and stand 35 inches (90 cm) high at the shoulder. These giants were named for the monastery (religious community) of Saint Bernard in the Swiss Alps. In the 1600s, members of the monastery used the dogs to rescue people buried beneath avalanches. The Saint Bernards were well suited for this work. The dogs are big and strong enough to move through deep snow. Their thick coats of hair keep them warm. Saint Bernards also have a good sense of smell, which helps them locate people.

Passing Through

The Alps form a barrier between southern and central Europe. In ancient times, when people wanted to travel from one side of the Alps to the other, they had to take passes, or paths, through the mountains. The journey on foot over rugged mountains could be treacherous. In winter, passes were often blocked with snow.

In 218 B.C., Hannibal, a general from the city of Carthage in North Africa, made history. Hannibal led an army of 38,000 foot soldiers, 8,000 soldiers on horseback, and 37 war elephants across the Alps to attack the Roman Empire. The Romans were shocked to see such a large army—and elephants—crossing the Alps.

This woodcut shows Hannibal and his army crossing the Alps to invade Rome in 218 B.C. It was published in a book on world history in 1882.

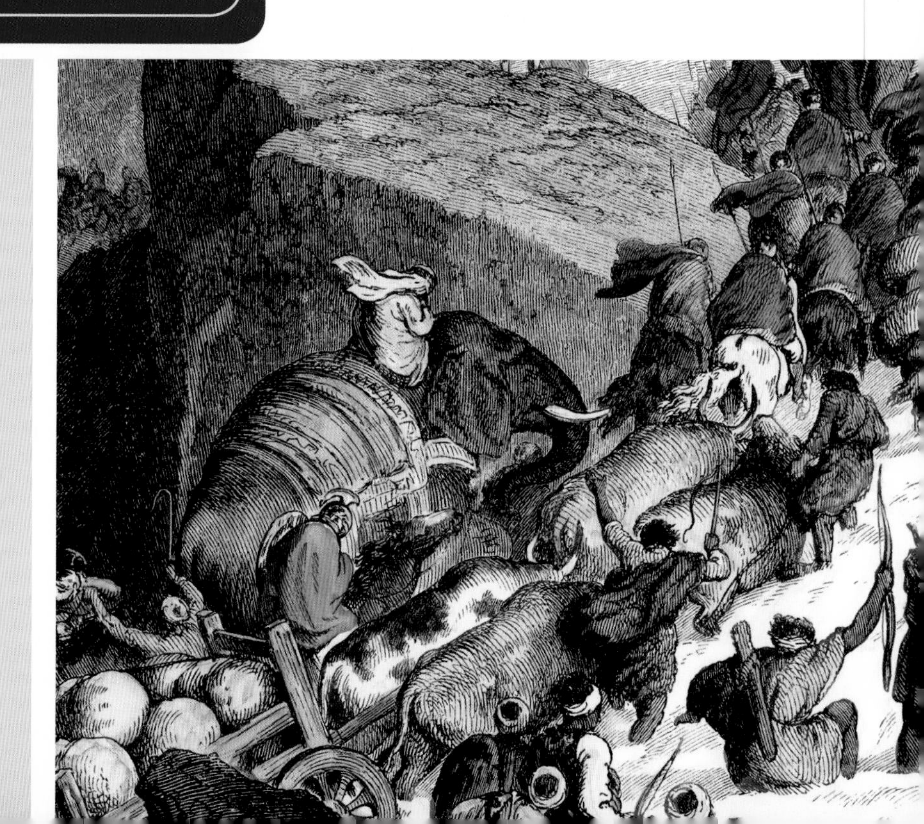

In modern times, it's much easier to cross the Alps. Workers have built roads and railroads across the mountains. In some places, they have dug tunnels through the rock. Cars and trains regularly travel from one side of the Alps to the other.

A train passes into a tunnel in a mountain in the Swiss Alps. Railroads make it easy to travel from one side of the mountain chain to the other.

Worries about the Wonder

Earth's climate is getting warmer. Many scientists think that pollutants from factories and cars are to blame. Those pollutants trap heat from the sun like the panes of glass in a greenhouse.

In the Alps and other places, scientists are recording record-high temperatures. The high temperatures are melting ice in Alpine glaciers. The glaciers are shrinking. High temperatures are also melting mountain snow. In some places, beautiful white snowcaps have disappeared.

Warmer weather in the Alps will affect people. Less snow might mean that fewer tourists come to the Alps to ski. Ski resorts, restaurants, hotels, and shops rely on tourism to make money. With less tourism, there will be fewer jobs for local people.

Global warming may also change the kinds of trees and other plants that grow on mountain slopes and valleys. Some Alpine trees do not grow well in warm temperatures. Those trees may die out as temperatures rise. As the trees die out, the animals that make their homes there may also disappear.

"We are currently experiencing the warmest period in the Alpine region in 1,300 years."

—Reinhard Boehm, Austrian scientist, 2006

The Alps *Grow Up*

The Alps are getting a tiny bit higher every year. They are growing because of global warming. As glaciers on the mountains melt and get smaller, there is less weight pressing down on the mountains. With that weight gone, Earth's crust springs back up. Scientists say that some Alpine mountains are growing about 0.035 inches (0.1 cm) per year. In fifty years, they will be about 1.8 inches (4.6 cm) taller.

The Alps rise behind Lake Seeben in Austria. The lower slopes of the mountains are covered with trees and other plants, while the top is cold and covered in snow.

Choose an Eighth Wonder

Now that you've read about the seven natural wonders of Europe, do a little research to choose an eighth wonder. You may enjoy working with a friend.

To do your research, look at some of the websites and books listed on pages 76 and 77. Look for places in Europe that

- ***are especially large***
- ***are exceptionally beautiful***
- ***were unknown to foreigners for many centuries***
- ***are unlike any other place on Earth***

You might even try gathering photos and writing your own chapter on the eighth wonder!

Timeline

218 B.C. Carthaginian general Hannibal leads an army, including war elephants, across the Alps. His Roman enemies are shocked to see elephants crossing the mountains.

50s B.C. Julius Caesar leads the Roman army through the Black Forest. He describes unusual animals living in the forest.

A.D. 565 According to legend, Saint Columba frightens away a sea monster near Loch Ness.

874 People from Norway build the first settlement on Iceland. They use Irish slaves to help build the settlement.

958 Harold Bluetooth unites Denmark into a single kingdom.

1750 Franz Anton Ketterer, a Black Forest clockmaker, makes the first cuckoo clock.

1810–1811 Mary Anning and her brother Joseph discover the fossilized skeleton of an ichthyosaur on the Jurassic Coast.

1812 Jacob and Wilhelm Grimm publish their first book of German fairy tales. Many of the stories are set in the Black Forest.

1823 Mary Anning discovers the remains of a plesiosaur on the Jurassic Coast.

1828 Mary Anning finds the skeleton of a dinosaur called *Dimorphodon* on the Jurassic Coast.

1933 George Spicer and his wife spot a monster on the road near Loch Ness. This is the first modern-day Nessie sighting.

1934 A British newspaper prints a photograph of a monster swimming in Loch Ness.

1963 An undersea volcano rises up to the ocean's surface near Iceland. The volcano creates Surtsey Island.

1967 The volcano beneath Surtsey Island stops erupting.

1973 The Eldfell Volcano erupts on Heimaey Island, one of the Westmann Islands. Lava destroys part of the town of Heimaey.

EARLY 1990s An old man reveals that the famous 1934 Loch Ness monster photo was made as a hoax.

1999 A fierce storm knocks down thousands of trees in the Black Forest.

2000 Fossil hunters discover bones from a dinosaur called *Scelidosaurus* on the Jurassic Coast. In the following years, other fossil hunters find more pieces, until the skeleton is complete.

2001 The Jurassic Coast becomes a UNESCO World Heritage Site.

2005 People on Heimaey Island begin the Pompeii of the North project. They excavate buildings buried by the Eldfell Volcano. UNESCO selects Geirangerfjord and Naeroyfjord in Norway as World Heritage Sites.

2007 One million pounds (454,000 kg) of chalk fall off Mons Klint during a landslide.

2008 Surtsey Island becomes a UNESCO World Heritage Site.

Glossary and Pronunciation Guide

acid rain: rain or snow mixed with acid from air pollution

coccolithophore: koh-koh-LIHTH-oh-for

continents: the seven giant landmasses on Earth. The continents are Africa, Antarctica, Asia, Australia, Europe, North America, and South America.

Cretaceous: kruh-TAY-shuhs

Dimorphodon*:* deye-MAWR-fuh-dahn

erode: to wear away rock and soil. Wind, rain, rivers, and other natural processes are responsible for most erosion.

fjord (FEE-ORD): a long, narrow inlet of the sea

fossils: remains, impressions, or traces of plants or animals from prehistoric times, usually preserved in rock

Geirangerfjord: GAY-rahng-yur-fyawrd

geothermal energy: energy created by heat beneath Earth's surface

glacier: a large body of ice moving slowly across the land

global warming: an increase in Earth's average temperatures. Most scientists think that air pollution is causing global warming.

Gondwanaland: gawn-DWAH-neh-land

Hardangerfjord: HAHR-dahng-yur-fyawrd

Heimaey: HAY-meye

ice age: a period in Earth's history when temperatures were cold and glaciers covered large areas of land

ichthyosaur: IK-thee-uh-sawr

Jurassic: juh-RA-sihk

landslide: the rapid movement of a mass of rock, dirt, or another substance down a hillside or mountainside

Laurasia: law-RAY-zhuh

loch: LAHK

magma: melted rock beneath Earth's surface

Mesozoic: meh-zoh-ZOH-ihk

Naeroyfjord: NAIR-oy-fyawrd

Pangaea: pan-JEE-uh

plesiosaur: PLEE-see-uh-sawr

Scelidosaurus*:* skeh-lih-dih-SAWR-uhs

Sognefjord: SAWNG-nuh-fyawrd

Surtsey: SUHRT-see

tectonic plates: giant slabs of rock that form Earth's crust

Triassic: treye-A-sihk

Vestmannaeyjar: VEHST-mahn-nah-AY-yahr

volcano: an opening in Earth's surface through which melted rock and gases occasionally burst forth

Source Notes

8 Alan Parker, "Guardian of the Loch," *Toronto Sun*, September 24, 2007, 8.

12 PBS, "The Beast of Loch Ness: Eyewitness Accounts," *Nova Online*, November 2000, http://pbs.org/wgbh/nova/lochness/eyewitness.html (March 8, 2008).

16 Jelle Zeilinga De Boer and Donald Theodore Sanders, *Volcanoes in Human History: The Far-Reaching Effects of Major Eruptions* (Princeton, NJ: Princeton University Press, 2002), 128.

18 Ibid., 116.

30 *Independent* (London), "UN May Give Heritage Site Status to Britain's Unique 'Jurassic Coast.'" December 4, 2001, 13.

33 BBC, "Landslip Is Worst in 100 Years." *BBC News Channel*, May 7, 2008, http://news.bbc.co.uk/go/pr/fr/-/2/hi/uk_news/england/dorset/7386923.stm (September 24, 2008).

39 Gaius Julius Caesar, "Commentaries on the Gallic War," *Corpus Scriptorum Latinorum*, 2007, http://www.forumromanum.org/literature/caesar/gallic_e6.html (February 24, 2008).

42 John Dornberg, "Germany's White Forest," *New York Times*, February 9, 1986, Travel section, 1.

46 Erik Pontoppidan, "Landscapes of Denmark," *ponty.dk*, 2008, http://www.ponty.dk/photos03.htm (July 17, 2008).

49 "Welcome to Insula Moenia," *Insula-moenia.dk*, 2007, http://www.insula-moenia.dk/ (July 17, 2008).

54 United Nations, "West Norwegian Fjords—Geirangerfjord and Nærøyfjord," *UNESCO World Heritage Center*, 2008, http://whc.unesco.org/en/list1195 (January 29, 2008).

56 Henry Armstrong, "In the Wonderland of Norway's Fjords," *New York Times*, September 18, 1927, SM 16.

67 Jona Lendering, "Hannibal in the Alps," *Livius*, 1998, http://www.livius.org/ha-hd/hannibal/alps_text.html (February 26, 2008).

70 Dara Brown, "Alps Experiencing Warmest Time in 1,300 years," *msnbc*, December 5, 2006, http://www.msnbc.msn.com/id/16052360 (March 31, 2008).

Selected Bibliography

Barnes-Svarney, Patricia L. *The Oryx Guide to Natural History: The Earth and All Its Inhabitants.* Phoenix: Oryx Press, 1999.

Blouet, Brian W. *The EU and Neighbors: A Geography of Europe in the Modern World.* Hoboken, NJ: Wiley, 2007.

Cleare, John. *Mountains of the World.* San Diego: Thunder Bay Press, 1997.

De Boer, Jelle Zeilinga, and Donald Theodore Sanders. *Volcanoes in Human History: The Far-Reaching Effects of Major Eruptions.* Princeton, NJ: Princeton University Press, 2002.

Gates, Alexander E., and David Ritchie. *Encyclopedia of Earthquakes and Volcanoes.* New York: Checkmark Books, 2007.

Hanbury-Tenison, Robin. *The Oxford Book of Exploration.* Oxford, UK: Oxford University Press, 1993.

Hancock, Paul, and Brian J. Skinner, ed. *The Oxford Companion to the Earth.* Oxford: Oxford University Press, 2000.

Luhr, James F., ed. *Earth.* London: Dorling Kindersley, 2003.

Man, John, and Chris Schuler. *The New Traveler's Atlas.* Hauppage, NY: Barron's Educational Services, 2007.

Moore, Robert J., Jr. *Natural Wonders of the World.* New York: Abbeville Press, 2000.

Shoumatoff, Nicholas, and Nina Shoumatoff. *The Alps: Europe's Mountain Heart.* Ann Arbor: University of Michigan Press, 2001.

Further Reading and Websites

Braun, Eric. *Norway in Pictures.* Minneapolis: Twenty-First Century Books, 2003. Norway is a breathtaking land, full of rugged mountains and thick forests. Most awe-inspiring of all are the fjords that line Norway's coast. This book examines Norway's geography, as well as its history and culture.

Goodhue, Thomas W. *Curious Bones: Mary Anning and the Birth of Paleontology.* Greensboro, NC: Morgan Reynolds Publishing, 2002. Mary Anning, a self-trained fossil hunter, earned a living collecting and selling fossils on the Jurassic Coast. She found the bones of previously unknown dinosaurs and earned a reputation as one of the world's greatest fossil hunters. This book tells her story.

Herbst, Judith. *Hoaxes.* Minneapolis: Lerner Publications Company, 2005. This book details the stories behind elaborate tricks, including a chapter on the Loch Ness monster. See who falls for these hoaxes and if you could have seen these tales as fake.

Lasky, Kathryn. *Surtsey: The Newest Place on Earth.* New York: Hyperion Books, 1992. The crew of the fishing boat *Isleifur II* witnessed the birth of the volcanic island Surtsey on November 14, 1963. Lasky explains the dynamic energy that creates volcanoes. She includes incredible photographs of the eruption.

McMillan, Bruce. *Nights of the Pufflings.* Boston: Houghton Mifflin, 1995. The island of Heimaey in Iceland is a special place. Not only is it a volcanic island, but it is also a place where children rescue fallen puffins and release them back into the sea. This book describes the rescue efforts with text and photos.

Spyri, Johanna. *Heidi.* 1881. Reprint, New York: Sterling Publishing, 2006. This classic children's book from 1881 tells the story of Heidi, a girl who lives with her grandfather in the Swiss Alps.

Verne, Jules. *A Journey to the Center of the Earth.* 1864. Reprint, New York: Sterling, 2007. In this classic science fiction novel, Professor Lidenbrock finds a medieval note. It tells of a passage to the center of Earth through a volcano in Iceland. Travel through the volcano along with the professor and his nephew.

Woods, Michael, and Mary B. Woods. *Avalanches.* Minneapolis: Lerner Publications Company, 2007. Avalanches can happen in any mountainous area, but the Alps are a prime avalanche spot. This book explains how avalanches form and tells how they have affected people.

Zuehlke, Jeffrey. *Germany in Pictures.* Minneapolis: Twenty-First Century Books, 2003. This comprehensive title tells all about the German landscape, including the magical Black Forest. The book also examines Germany's history, culture, and people.

Websites

The Beast of Loch Ness

http://www.pbs.org/wgbh/nova/lochness/

Is Nessie fact or fiction? This website, a companion to a 1999 television show, sets out to answer the question.

The Four Fjord Counties

http://www.fjords.com/

This travel website offers loads of information on Norway's fjords, including breathtaking pictures.

Hiking the Alps from End to End

http://www.nationalgeographic.com/adventure/travel/alps/alps.html

Follow French chemical engineer Maurice Chazalet on his three-month journey through the Alps.

Jurassic Coast: Dorset and East Devon World Heritage Site

http://www.jurassiccoast.com/

This site provides a thorough overview of Earth's history over the last 250 million years. It includes information on the geology, history, climate, and ecology of the Jurassic Coast.

Volcano World

http://volcano.und.edu

This site explores volcanoes in detail. You can even watch actual footage of the Eldfell explosion in 1973.

Index

About the Authors

Michael Woods is a science and medical journalist in Washington, D.C. He has won many national writing awards. Mary B. Woods is a school librarian. Their past books include the eight-volume Ancient Technology series and the Disasters Up Close series. The Woodses have four children. When not writing, reading, or enjoying their grandchildren, the Woodses travel to gather material for future books.

Photo Acknowledgments

The images in this book are used with the permission of: © iStockphoto.com/Tom De Bruyne, p. 5; © Tom Stoddart Archive/Hulton Archive/Getty Images, p. 6; © Laura Westlund/Independent Picture Service, pp. 7, 15, 27, 37, 45, 53, 63; © Emory Kristof/National Geographic/Getty Images, p. 8; © Simon Price/Alamy, p. 10; © Keystone/Hulton Archive/Getty Images, p. 11; © jeremy sutton-hibbert/Alamy, p. 12; © iStockphoto.com/S. Greg Panosian, p. 13; © Ragnar Larusson/Photo Researchers, Inc., p. 14; © Ernst Haas/Premium Archive/Getty Images, p. 17 (top); © ARCTIC IMAGES/Alamy, pp. 17 (bottom), 24; © Frans Lemmens/Iconica/Getty Images, p. 19; © Hemis.fr/SuperStock, p. 20; © Pete Turner/The Image Bank/Getty Images, pp. 21 (top), 22; © Nordicphotos/Alamy, p. 21 (bottom); © Cyril Ruoso/JH Editorial/Minden Pictures/Getty Images, p. 23; © age fotostock/SuperStock, pp. 25, 44; © Jinny Goodman/Photographer's Choice RR/Getty Images, p. 26; © The Natural History Museum, London, pp. 28, 31, 32 (both); © The British Library/HIP/The Image Works, p. 29; © Frank Siteman/Science Faction/Getty Images, pp. 30 (top), 33, 72 (center right); © Derek Croucher/Alamy, p. 30 (bottom); © Colin Palmer Photography/Alamy, p. 34; © Guy Edwardes/Photographer's Choice/Getty Images, p. 35; © iStockphoto.com/Richard Goerg, p. 36; © Armand-Photo-Nature/Alamy, p. 38; © Nick & Janet Wiseman/Art Directors & TRIP, p. 40; © Juniors Bildarchiv/Alamy, p. 41 (top); © Travel Ink/Digital Vision/Getty Images, p. 41 (bottom); © Christian Teubner/StockFood Creative/Getty Images, p. 42; © Sigrid Dauth Stock Photography/Alamy, p. 43 (top); © Arco Images GmbH/Alamy, p. 43 (bottom); © LOOK Die Bildagentur der Fotografen GmbH/Alamy, p. 46; © Andrew Syred/Photo Researchers, Inc., p. 47; © Stockbyte/Getty Images, p. 48 (top);© Don Klumpp/Photographer's Choice/Getty Images, p. 48 (bottom); © iStockphoto.com/Tina Lorien, pp. 50, 72 (bottom left); © Marco Cristofori/Robert Harding World Imagery/Getty Images, p. 51; © Pal Hermansen/Stone/Getty Images, p. 52; © Art Kowalsky/Alamy, p. 55 (top); © Arnulf Husmo/Stone/Getty Images, pp. 55 (bottom), 72 (top left); © Bob Langrish/Dorling Kindersley/Getty Images, p. 56; © A C Waltham/Robert Harding World Imagery/Getty Images, p. 57; © North Wind Picture Archives, pp. 58 (top), 69; © iStockphoto.com/Tomas Navratil, p. 58 (bottom); © nagelestock.com/Alamy, p. 59; © T. Waltham/Robert Harding World Imagery/Getty Images, p. 60; © Travel Ink/Gallo Images/Getty Images, p. 61; © SuperStock, Inc./SuperStock, p. 62; © Cyril Isy-Schwart/The Image Bank/Getty Images, p. 64; © Prisma/SuperStock, p. 65; © Luis Castaneda Inc./Riser/Getty Images, p. 66 (left); © J Melhuish/Art Directors & TRIP, p. 66 (right); © A.A.M. Van der Heyden/Independent Picture Service, p. 67; © Hauke Dressler/LOOK/Getty Images, p. 68; © Taylor S. Kennedy/National Geographic/Getty Images, p. 70; © Andreas Strauss/LOOK/Getty Images, p. 71; © Stephen Studd/Stone/Getty Images, p. 72 (top center); © Patrick Dieudonne/Robert Harding World Imagery/Getty Images, p. 72 (top right); © Sigurgeir Jonasson/Nordic Photos/Getty Images, p. 72 (bottom center); © Damian Davies/Photographer's Choice/Getty Images, p. 72 (bottom right).

Front Cover: © iStockphoto.com/Tina Lorien (top left); © Stephen Studd/Stone/Getty Images (top center); © Patrick Dieudonne/Robert Harding World Imagery/Getty Images (top right); © Sigurgeir Jonasson/Nordic Photos/Getty Images (center); © Arnulf Husmo/Stone/Getty Images (bottom left); © Frank Siteman/Science Faction/Getty Images (bottom center); © Damian Davies/Photographer's Choice/Getty Images (bottom right).

SUMMIT FREE PUBLIC LIBRARY